KIDS LOVE ART CRAFTS

Joanna Ponto and Heather Miller

Enslow Publishing
101 W. 23rd Street
Suite 240
New York, NY 10011
USA

enslow.com

Published in 2019 by Enslow Publishing, LLC.
101 W. 23rd Street, Suite 240, New York, NY 10011

Library of Congress Cataloging-in-Publication Data

Names: Ponto, Joanna, author. | Miller, Heather, author.

Title: Kids love art crafts / Joanna Ponto and Heather Miller.

Description: New York : Enslow Publishing, 2019. | Series: Kids love crafts | Audience: Grades 3-5. | Includes bibliographical references and index.

Identifiers: LCCN 2018008243| ISBN 9781978501973 (library bound) | ISBN 9781978502772 (pbk.) | ISBN 9781978502789 (6 pack)

Subjects: LCSH: Handicraft—Juvenile literature.

Classification: LCC TT160 .P638 2019 | DDC 745.5—dc23

LC record available at https://lccn.loc.gov/2018008243

Printed in the United States of America

To Our Readers: We have done our best to make sure all website addresses in this book were active and appropriate when we went to press. However, the author and the publisher have no control over and assume no liability for the material available on those websites or on any websites they may link to. Any comments or suggestions can be sent by email to customerservice@enslow.com.

Portions of this book originally appeared in *Nifty Thrifty Art Crafts*.

Photo Credits: Crafts on cover and throughout book prepared by June Ponte; photography by Nicole DiMella/Enslow Publishing, LLC; p. 5 JEAN-PIERRE MULLER/AFP/Getty Images; p. 26 PIERRE ANDRIEU/AFP/Getty Images (upper left), Paolo Gallo/Shutterstock.com (upper right), WitR/Shutterstock.com (center left), China Photos/Getty Images News/Getty Images (bottom right), Fine Art Images/SuperStock/Getty Images (bottom left); p. 27 Daderot/Wikimedia Commons/String bag, dog teeth, Papua New Guinea, 1890 Staatlichen Museums für Völkerkunde München DSC08306.JPG/public domain (upper left), DEA PICTURE LIBRARY/De Agostini Picture Library/Getty Images (upper right), NELSON ALMEIDA/AFP/Getty Images (center left), Carl Court/Getty Images News/Getty Images (bottom right), PATRICK KOVARIK/AFP/Getty Images (bottom left); design elements on cover and throughout book: Betelgejze/Shutterstock.com (series logo), Chinch/Shutterstock.com (torn rainbow paper border), daisybee/Shutterstock.com (colorful letters), Iuliia Aseeva/Shutterstock.com ("love" in series and book titles), Yulia M./Shutterstock.com (colorful numbers).

SAFETY NOTE:

Be sure to **ask for help from an adult**, if needed, to complete these crafts!

CONTENTS

ART THROUGHOUT THE AGES

People use art to express themselves in beautiful ways for others to see. Art has been an important part of human society since prehistoric times. The oldest known piece of art is a cave painting of a red disk from El Castillo, in Spain. It is thought to be 40,800 years old! Since then, people have developed different forms of art using a wide variety of materials and subjects.

Ancient Greeks sculpted statues of their gods from marble and bronze. The ancient Chinese painted landscapes that also featured calligraphy, the art of handwriting. Native Americans wove colorful blankets and carved totem poles, wood posts with symbols or figures. In Africa, people made animal masks from wood to use in religious ceremonies.

During the Renaissance (1300s–1600s) in Europe, people became interested in ancient Roman and Greek art. They moved away from the religious subjects of the Middle Ages (c. 500–1500) and focused more on mythology, history, and daily life. Famous artists of this period include Italian painters Michelangelo (1475–1564) and Leonardo da Vinci (1452–1519).

In the late 1800s, Impressionism began in France by Claude Monet (1840–1926). These artists wanted to capture the moment, the light and color of a scene, instead of the details of the object. They painted everyday subjects, often outdoors.

Postmodernism describes the era we're in now. It includes digital art, installation art, and video art. Postmodernism goes against the idea that a work of art has only one meaning, decided by the artist when he or she made the piece. Viewers can come up with their own ideas of what the artwork is trying to say.

Each craft in this book is inspired by a real-life work of art. Learn fascinating facts and create fun projects you can share with family and friends!

Mona Lisa **by Leonardo da Vinci is the most famous painting in the world. It was created in the early 1500s and now hangs in the Louvre Museum in Paris, France.**

PREHISTORIC PLACE MATS

In 2014, researchers figured out that a cave painting on the island of Sulawesi in Indonesia was at least 35,400 years old. This makes it one of the oldest examples of figurative art (art representing real-life objects) in the world. The painting is of an animal called a pig deer. Animals are often drawn in cave paintings. Design your own prehistoric symbol to make place mats.

WHAT YOU WILL NEED:

- brown paper bag
- crayons
- paper bowl
- measuring cup
- teaspoon
- water
- black poster paint
- paintbrush
- newspapers
- paper towels
- construction paper
- white glue

WHAT TO DO:

1 Tear a section from a brown paper bag. The ragged edges will give the paper a prehistoric look.

2 Using crayons, create your own prehistoric design.

3 Crumple your drawing and squeeze it gently under running water. Carefully open the paper to reveal a web of wrinkles. Let dry.

 4 To make your drawing look even more prehistoric, make a paint wash of ½ cup water and one teaspoon of black poster paint. If you wish, also use brown poster paint.

 5 Brush the mixture over your drawing. The crayon will resist, or push, the paint away, letting your design show through. Excess paint can be blotted away with a paper towel. Let dry on a small stack of paper towels or newspapers.

6 Glue the drawing to a piece of construction paper. Let dry. Then, make a set to use as place mats for a prehistoric feast!

PERSONAL HIEROGLYPH

Ancient Egyptians developed hieroglyphs to communicate. Hieroglyphs are pictures and symbols that represent sounds. Combining these symbols created words. Some symbols were figures of animals. Others were of everyday objects. Still others would just be shapes. For example, a lion represented the letter L, a lasso symbolized an O, and a zigzag stood for N. Create your own unique hieroglyph that represents you!

WHAT TO DO:

1 Begin by writing a list of words that describe you. Use the words as an inspiration for your personal symbol. Spend some time sketching ideas. Once you decide on a symbol, draw it carefully on a clean sheet of paper. (For the symbol shown, see page 30.)

WHAT YOU WILL NEED:

- pencil
- sketch paper
- white paper
- aluminum foil
- old magazine or newspapers
- crayon
- scissors
- an empty cereal box
- clear tape
- pipe cleaners

2 Tear off a sheet of aluminum foil the same size as your drawing. Place the foil on top of an old magazine or newspaper.

 3 Lay your drawing on top of the foil. Draw over your design with a crayon or pencil. Do not press too hard or you will break through the foil.

 4 Remove the paper. Turn the foil over to reveal your design.

5 Leave a 1-inch (2½-centimeter) border around your design. Cut off the rest of the foil. Cut a piece of light cardboard a little smaller than your foil design. Wrap the foil around the cardboard. If needed, use clear tape to tape the foil to the cardboard.

6 Tape pipe cleaners to the back of the cardboard around the outside. Bend each pipe cleaner into an interesting shape. Display on your bedroom door or wall.

PYRAMID PAPERWEIGHT

Although many ancient cultures built pyramids, the Pyramids of Giza in Egypt are probably the most well known. These three pyramids were built about 4,500 years ago as tombs for the Egyptian rulers, or pharaohs, Khufu, Khafre, and Menkaure. Khufu's pyramid, called the Great Pyramid, is the largest at about 481 feet (147 meters) tall. It's made up of more than two million stone blocks. Build a much smaller and lighter pyramid of your own with cardboard and sandpaper.

WHAT YOU WILL NEED:

- paper
- pencil
- ruler
- sandpaper
- scissors
- crayons or markers
- an empty cereal box
- a small rock
- clear tape
- tacky craft glue

WHAT TO DO:

1 Draw a triangle on paper with all three sides measuring 3 inches (7½ cm) (see **A**). (See page 28 for the pattern.)

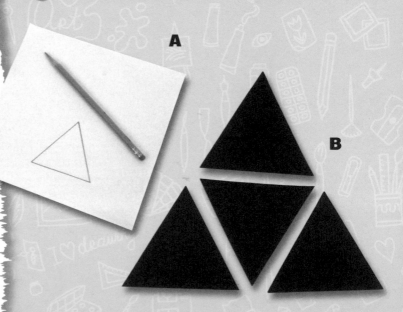

A

B

10

2 Use the paper triangle as a pattern to trace four triangles onto the smooth side of sandpaper. Cut them out (see **B**).

3 Using crayons or markers, decorate the rough side of each triangle with Egyptian symbols (see **C**). (See page 30 for some symbols, or make your own.)

C

4 Use the paper triangle to trace four triangles onto the cardboard. Cut them out.

D

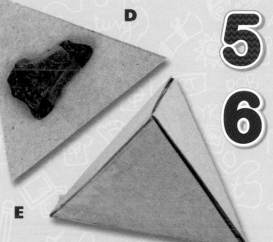

E

5 Tape a small rock to one of the cardboard triangles (see **D**). This is the base of the pyramid.

6 Place the other cardboard triangles around the base. Secure them to the base with clear tape. If you wish, before you seal the pyramid closed, write a secret or a wish on a small piece of paper. Tuck the paper inside your pyramid.

7 Fold up the triangle around the base (see **E**). Tape them together.

8 Use tacky craft glue to glue the decorative sandpaper triangles to the outside of the cardboard pyramid (see **F**). Let dry. (White glue will melt the sandpaper.)

F

9 Make several pyramids and display them together to create your own Egyptian desert.

RECYCLED PAPER WINDOW DECORATION

Before the invention of paper in 105 CE, people in China wrote on bone, bamboo, or silk. Cai Lun (50–121 CE) was a servant of the imperial court who is credited as the inventor of paper and the papermaking process. He made paper from tree bark, hemp, old rags, and fish nets by pounding them into a sheet. This material was easier to carry around than bone or bamboo and much cheaper than silk. You can experience the papermaking process yourself with this project!

WHAT YOU WILL NEED:

- old newspapers
- scissors
- large bowl
- measuring cup
- water
- food coloring
- wooden spoon
- can opener
- two empty tin cans, close to the same size
- small scrap of window screen, burlap, or plastic canvas (Ask permission first!)
- shallow pan or plastic tray
- glitter (optional)
- paper towels
- hole punch
- string or yarn

WHAT TO DO:

1 Tear or cut one sheet of newspaper into tiny pieces, about the size of small coins (see **A**).

A

2 Put the small pieces of newspaper into a large bowl and cover with about 4 cups (1 liter) of warm water. Be sure all the paper is soaked in water. You may need to add more water later since the paper will absorb it quickly.

3 Add several drops of food coloring to the mixture and stir. Let the paper mixture sit for a few hours. It is done when it is nice and mushy.

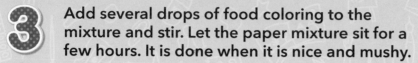

B

4 **Ask an adult** to help you remove both ends from two empty cans (see **B**). (Each can should be open like a tube.)

5 Cut a square of window screen, burlap, or plastic canvas just large enough to cover the top of one can.

6 Place one can inside the shallow pan or plastic tray. Set the screen on top of the can. Stack the second can on top of the screen (see **C**).

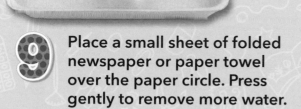

C

7 Scoop ¼ cup of the paper pulp out of the bowl and carefully pour it into the top can. If you wish, sprinkle the pulp with glitter.

8 Wait for most of the water to drain (see **D**). Carefully lift away the top can.

D

9 Place a small sheet of folded newspaper or paper towel over the paper circle. Press gently to remove more water.

10 Lift the newspaper and paper circle from the screen and can. Set it in a safe place to dry. Once dry, carefully peel the paper circle from the newspaper.

11 Carefully punch a hole in the top. Thread with string or yarn and hang in a window (see **E**).

E

RELIEF PRINT

The Japanese artist Katsushika Hokusai (1760–1849) created more than thirty thousand prints and drawings between 1779 and 1849. He used a form of printmaking called relief printing. First, you carve an image into a surface such as wood or foam. Next, you apply ink or paint to the surface. Then, you press the carved plate onto paper. You can use the same carved plate to make multiple prints. Create a journal cover, greeting cards, place mats, or artwork to hang on your wall. The possibilities are endless!

WHAT YOU WILL NEED:

- construction paper
- journal (optional)
- scissors
- foam meat or cheese tray, washed and dried
- dull pencil
- paintbrush
- poster paint
- white glue

WHAT TO DO:

1 Sketch a design on a piece of construction paper that is the same size as your journal cover (see **A**). (See page 29 for the pattern.) If you do not have a journal, use an old or new notebook.

A

2 Cut the sides off a foam tray to make one flat piece.

3 Place the sketched design on the smooth side of the foam. Use a dull pencil to press firmly as you draw over the design. The pencil should leave an imprint of your design in the foam (see **B**).

B

4 Apply an even layer of poster paint over the design (see **C**). Turn the tray over, paint side down, onto a new piece of construction paper. Press firmly with the palms of both hands.

C

5 Carefully peel the paper away to reveal the design. Let dry.

6 Glue the print to the cover of your journal. If you wish, add to your design (see **D**). Let dry.

7 Make several prints. Experiment with color. Try mixing two colors of paint. Let dry.

JOURNAL

D

TEXTURED POUCH

Purses and pouches have been carried by both men and women since prehistoric times. The earliest bags were made from animal skin or plant fibers. People used them to carry weapons, tools, food, and other important items. Researchers believe they found the world's oldest purse in a Stone Age grave in Germany. The bag was decorated with more than a hundred dog teeth. Many cultures used animal teeth, fur, feathers, beads, embroidery, jewels, and other items to decorate their bags. Create your own textured pouch, then use it to collect interesting things you find on your next hike.

WHAT YOU WILL NEED:

- scissors
- an empty cereal box
- poster paint (optional)
- paintbrush (optional)
- ruler
- pencil
- hole punch
- yarn
- old shoelaces (optional)
- white glue
- leaves, seeds, grass, beads
- zipper top bag

WHAT TO DO:

1 Cut one large side from an empty cereal box. Fold the cardboard in half so the inside shows (see **A**). Unfold. If you wish, use poster paint to paint the inside of the cardboard. Let dry.

A

2 With a pencil and ruler, make 5 to 6 "**x**" marks on two short sides. Make them evenly spaced. Fold the cardboard. Make "**x**" marks on the other two short sides so the marks line up. Use a hole punch to carefully punch out the "**x**" marks. The holes should match up when the cardboard is folded. Make sure the plain or painted side is showing (see **B**).

B

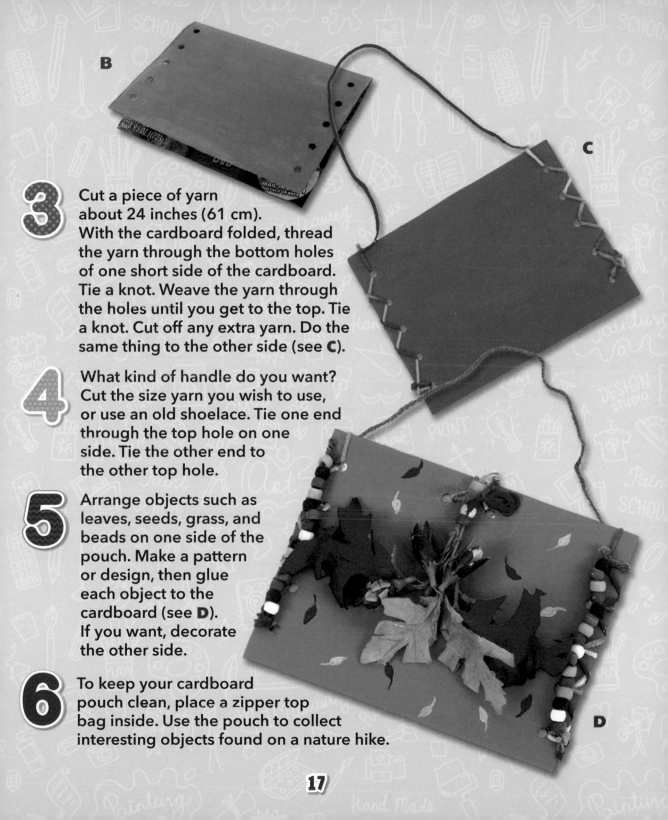

3 Cut a piece of yarn about 24 inches (61 cm). With the cardboard folded, thread the yarn through the bottom holes of one short side of the cardboard. Tie a knot. Weave the yarn through the holes until you get to the top. Tie a knot. Cut off any extra yarn. Do the same thing to the other side (see **C**).

C

4 What kind of handle do you want? Cut the size yarn you wish to use, or use an old shoelace. Tie one end through the top hole on one side. Tie the other end to the other top hole.

5 Arrange objects such as leaves, seeds, grass, and beads on one side of the pouch. Make a pattern or design, then glue each object to the cardboard (see **D**). If you want, decorate the other side.

6 To keep your cardboard pouch clean, place a zipper top bag inside. Use the pouch to collect interesting objects found on a nature hike.

D

SEURAT POINTILLISM PICTURE

Pointillism is a style of painting that uses only small dots of pure color to create an entire picture. When you look at a pointillism painting from far away, the dots blend together and create a smooth image, just like pixels on a computer screen. Georges-Pierre Seurat (1859–1891) studied the science of colors and light to invent pointillism. This technique made artwork brighter and richer. Paint a unique portrait of yourself using pointillism.

WHAT YOU WILL NEED:

- close-up photograph of yourself
- pencil
- construction paper
- cotton swabs
- poster paint

WHAT TO DO:

1 Study your photograph. Use a pencil to draw a simple portrait on construction paper. Do not worry if it turns out looking a bit funny. It is art!

2 Dip the end of a cotton swab into poster paint. Fill in the portrait by stamping small dots with the cotton swab.

3 Use different colors to add more detail to your portrait. Let dry.

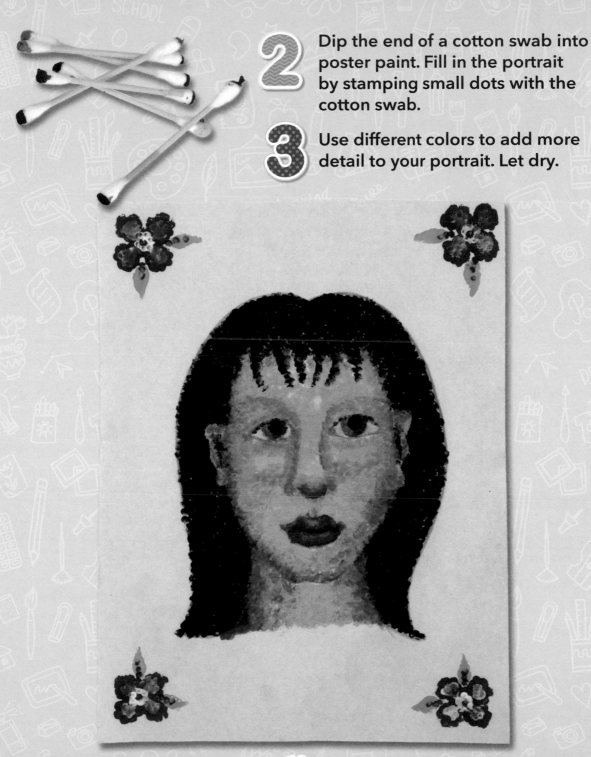

WARHOL POP ART STAMP

Pop art uses subjects from mass media and popular culture. It celebrates objects and people from everyday life. Andy Warhol (1928–1987) was one of the most famous Pop artists. He painted soup cans, soda bottles, movie star Marilyn Monroe, and other subjects most people would recognize. Use a regular sponge to create your own Warhol-inspired piece of Pop art.

WHAT YOU WILL NEED:

- marker
- new, clean kitchen sponge
- scissors
- ruler
- pencil
- construction paper
- poster paint

WHAT TO DO:

1 Decide on a simple shape such as a star, heart, circle, or triangle. (See page 28 for a heart pattern.) With a marker, draw the shape onto a new, clean kitchen sponge. Cut it out (see **A**).

A

2 Draw a grid on construction paper with a pencil and ruler so there are six spaces on the paper. Go over the lines with a marker (see **B**).

3 Choose six different colors of poster paint.

4 Dip the sponge into one color and stamp onto one space on the construction paper. Rinse the sponge. Make sure to wring out the water well. Dip the sponge into another color and stamp onto another space. Repeat this process until each space has a different color stamped shape (see **C**). Let dry.

B

C

5 Make more "pop art" with other shapes and other objects.

POLLOCK ABSTRACT ART PENCIL HOLDER

Abstract Expressionism is a form of art where the artist uses colors to express themselves. Many abstract pieces of art look like paint was just thrown or brushed onto the canvas without a specific subject in mind. This is exactly what Jackson Pollock (1912-1956) was famous for. He splashed, dripped, and flung paints onto canvas laid out on the floor. His work brought forth feelings of excitement and energy. Express yourself with this colorful project!

WHAT YOU WILL NEED:

- newspaper
- paper bowls
- poster paint
- white glue
- craft sticks
- white construction paper
- old toothbrush (Get permission first!)
- empty soup can, washed and dried
- ruler
- pencil
- scissors

WHAT TO DO:

1 Cover your workspace with newspaper.

2 Choose four different poster paint colors. Pour small amounts of each color into separate paper bowls. Pour about twice that amount of white glue into each paper bowl. Use craft sticks to stir the paint and glue mixture.

3 Place a piece of white construction paper on the newspapers in front of you. Dip an old toothbrush into one color. Lightly tap the top of the toothbrush, bristles side down, over the paper. Rinse the toothbrush off before going to the next color. Repeat the process for each color. Let dry.

4 Measure the width of paper needed to cover a soup can by laying the can down on the paper.

5 Use a ruler to draw a line down the length of the paper. Cut the paper along the pencil line. Roll the paper around the can and glue the edges. Let dry. Use the can to hold your colorful pencil collection!

CALDER MOBILE

A mobile is a sculpture that combines shape with balance. Objects are hung from rods with wire or string and move when touched or hit by air. How the different parts move is part of the art! Alexander Calder (1898-1976) was one of the first to create mobiles. He used bright colors and simple shapes for his designs. Use old computer CDs to make your own mobile. Hang it in an area with a slight breeze and watch it dance in the air!

WHAT YOU WILL NEED:

- wire clothes hanger
- ruler
- string
- scissors
- 5 old computer CDs (Ask permission first!)
- glitter (optional)
- beads (optional)
- white glue
- permanent markers
- paintbrush
- poster paint
- light cardboard
- aluminum foil

WHAT TO DO:

1 Use the hanger as a foundation for the mobile (see **A**).

2 Cut nine pieces of string of different lengths (ranging from 6 inches to 18 inches [15 to 46 cm]) and set aside.

3 Decorate five CDs with permanent markers, glitter, and beads. Let dry. Thread a piece of string through the center hole of each CD and tie (see **B**).

A

4 Cut cardboard into four interesting shapes. Tape one end of a piece of string to the back of each cardboard piece. Cover each shape with aluminum foil, leaving the rest of the string out. If you wish, use poster paint to decorate the foil shapes. Let dry.

B

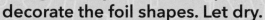

5 Tie the other end of all nine strings to the hanger. Try to balance your mobile so it will hang and move smoothly (see **C**).

C

REAL-LIFE INSPIRATIONS

All the crafts in this book were inspired by artwork from different time periods, cultures, and art movements. Check out what a cave drawing, relief print, pointillism painting, and the other subjects featured in this book really look like!

"Bull," Lascaux Cave, France
Prehistoric Place Mats, page 6

Egyptian Hieroglyphics
Personal Hieroglyph, page 8

Pyramids of Giza, Egypt
Pyramid Paperweight, page 10

Chinese Handmade Paper
Recycled Paper Window Decoration, page 12

Rainstorm Beneath the Summit (1831)
by Katsushika Hokusai
Relief Print, page 14

**Bag with dog teeth (1890),
Papua New Guinea**
Textured Pouch, page 16

*A Sunday Afternoon on the Island
of La Grande Jatte (1884)*
by Georges Seurat
Seurat Pointillism Picture, page 18

**Screen Prints of Marilyn Monroe
(1967) by Andy Warhol**
Warhol Pop Art Stamp, page 20

Blue Poles (1952)
by Jackson Pollock
Pollock Abstract Art
Pencil Holder, page 22

Horizontal (1974)
by Alexander Calder
Calder Mobile, page 24

PATTERNS

The percentages included on the patterns tell you how much to enlarge or shrink the image using a copier. (The patterns that say 100% are at the correct size as they are.) Most copiers and printers have an adjustable size/percentage feature to change the size of an image when you print it. After you print the patterns to their true sizes, cut them out or use tracing paper to copy them. **Ask an adult** to help you trace and cut the shapes.

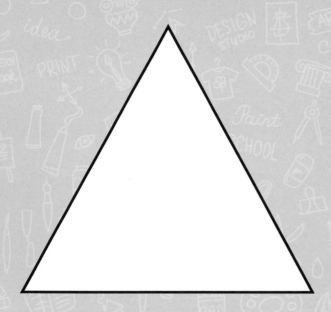

**Pyramid Paperweight
at 100%**

**Warhol Pop Art Stamp
at 100%**

Relief Print at 100%

Personal Hieroglyph at 100%

Learn More

Books

Azzita, Emanuele. *Origami Arts and Crafts*. New York, NY: Enslow Publishing, 2017.

Brooks, Susie. *Get into Art*. New York, NY: Kingfisher, 2018.

Brooks, Susie. *Printing and Stamping Art*. New York, NY: PowerKids Press, 2018.

Frisch, Cari, and Elizabeth Margulies. *Art Making with MoMA*. New York, NY: Museum of Modern Art, 2018.

Websites

DLTK's Crafts for Kids
www.dltk-kids.com/world/index.htm
These crafts and activities are inspired by countries and cultures from around the world.

Ducksters Art History and Artists for Kids
www.ducksters.com/history/art/
Read more about art movements, famous artists, and ancient art and explore art terms and a timeline of Western art.

PBS Crafts for Kids
www.pbs.org/parents/crafts-for-kids/
Learn to make crafts inspired by all different kinds of topics, such as a nebula jar, an egg carton seed start, and a paper cardinal.

INDEX